Aella Greene

Happy Days at Hampton

And Other Poems

Aella Greene

Happy Days at Hampton
And Other Poems

ISBN/EAN: 9783744704960

Printed in Europe, USA, Canada, Australia, Japan

Cover: Foto ©Thomas Meinert / pixelio.de

More available books at **www.hansebooks.com**

HAPPY DAYS

AT

HAMPTON

AND

OTHER POEMS.

BY

AELLA GREENE,

AUTHOR OF "RHYMES OF YANKEE LAND."

———•••———

SPRINGFIELD:
GILL & HAYES.
1872.

TO

Dr. J. G. Holland,

AND THE NOBLE MEN AND WOMEN INTO WHOSE SOCIETY I
HAVE BEEN LED BY FOLLOWING HIS TEACHINGS,

I Dedicate

"HAPPY DAYS AT HAMPTON,"

WISHING IT MORE ABLY PORTRAYED THE PRINCIPLES OF TRUE
CHIVALRY WHICH HE AND THEY ILLUSTRATE SO
WELL BY THEIR LIVES.

CONTENTS.

	PAGE.
INTRODUCTION, ...	11

PART FIRST.—HAMPTON:

A Welcome Funeral, ...	15
The Group, ...	18

PART SECOND.—JAMESON'S STORY:

The Waynes, ...	20
War Days Come, ...	23
"Do Thou, My Harry,"	24
Colonel Goodman and His Men, . .	26
In Goodman's Tent, ...	29

CONTENTS.

	PAGE.
GOODMAN SPEAKS TO STERNMAN,	30
A MEMORABLE DRESS PARADE,	35
THE FIGHT AT SUNSET,	36
"AND WITH HIS MUSKET EARNED A SWORD,"	37
HEAVEN'S BEST PLAN,	39
A TYRANT'S GRAVE,	40
THE EFFECT,	41

PART THIRD.—GOODMAN TO THE GROUP:

"EACH PLAN SUCCEEDS,"	43
TEMPERANCE AT HAMPTON,	44
A SCHOOL ON THE TAVERN SITE,	47
GOOD NIGHT,	49

PART FOURTH.—AT THE THANKSGIVING:

THE FACTORIES,	52
THE HAMPTON PAPER,	54

CONTENTS.

	PAGE.
A Church and a Lodge,	55
With all These Honors,	56
Mrs. John Goodman,	58
Bread on the Waters,	60
"With Circumspection, Let Us, Now,"	64
When Goodman Dies,"	65

OUR YANKEE LAND, ... 69

LOCAL LINES:

The Dead Doherty,	75
"Sam's" Paper,	78
Our Conductors,	82
The "River Road,"	85

SUMMER PLACES:

Barrington,	89

	PAGE.
TILDEN,	91
UP THE PASSUMPSIC,	93
"ISRAEL'S RIVER,"	95
THE AMMONOOSUC,	97

HAPPY DAYS AT HAMPTON.

INTRODUCTION.

OF Hampton's noble-hearted men,
    Theme worthy song of better pen,
The story is; and most I tell
How Goodman lived so grand and well,
And taught, by practice and by speech,
Important truth to live and teach:
"It bringeth bliss to bless the sad;
And saveth us to save the bad;
Dispensing riches brings us wealth;
Aid to the sick insures our health;
More than ourselves demand our care,
For we our brothers' keepers are."
In Hampton this John Goodman, best

Of all the men who Hampton blest,
Serenely lived, with honors high,
A happy home, and happy sky.
Though known in youth to want and pain,
He made his griefs his richest gain,
And by his graces, grit and skill,
Successful climbed life's sunny hill;
Then made and followed out a plan,
Always to bless his fellow man;
Remembering bread on waters cast
Returns again, increased, at last.
He often found the days were few
Ere he attested Scripture true;
His kindness found, redoubled, given
Into his hands, as if from heaven.

PART I.

HAMPTON.

THE place is fenced from eastern snows;
    On it but light the winter blows;
Hills crowned with oak, and elm, and beech,
Forbid the blasts those homes to reach.
Far up a glade a brook begins;
Through fields its merry progress wins;
Then plunges down a cascade bright,
And, onward flowing, gives delight
To Hampton glades that ever bear
Of all things good abundant share.

A flowery mead has purling springs,
Where singing birds do dip their wings.
Bright streamlets course the glades along;
Sweet undertones of grander song.
At times a breeze blows o'er the scene;
Then far forest belt and coppice green,
And gnarled oaks upon the hill,
Yielding as giants bend their will,
Unite with rill, and spring, and bird,
In hymn as grand as ear has heard.
Beyond the falls the village good
Extends a mile to belt of wood
That crowns an unpretending hill;
And dwellings there, and busy mill,
And church, and school, and village stores;
Fragrant of cattle and of chores,
The barns; indeed, the village all

Is shaded well with maples tall,

And beech, and birch, and "button-ball."

The grove upon the gentle hill

Has mossy spring and gurgling rill,

And rocks, and knoll, and pleasant dell,

And so it is adapted well

For squirrel haunts, and haunts of birds,

For lovers' walks and lovers' words.

And now as in the days of old,

Through summer heat and winter cold;

In greening spring and autumn brown,

It is a fine New England town.

A WELCOME FUNERAL.

The town we visit on a day

When useless dust is laid away,

Of one for whom none good could say;
The parson only "Let us pray!"
Flint Sternman was this hard man's name;
His father's cognomen the same.
How they were suffered there to dwell
Is more than I can truly tell.
The Hampton saints sought well a cure,
But did five decades Flint endure;
And when he died they thanked the Lord
For good fulfillment of His word,
That wicked men from earth are driven
To places far away from heaven.
No one in town would bearer be
"For such a cruel man as he."
But six young men whom he oppressed,
And from his hatred gave no rest,
Who forth from Hampton went, to find,

As luck would have it, fortune kind,

The day before the funeral day,

To Hampton came a call to pay;

And, being in a pleasant mood,

Proposed to do Flint's memory good.

"Let us keep Scripture, now," they said,

"Put coals of kindness on his head;

As he, thank God, at last is dead,

Let's kindly bear his form away

And close our hatred with the day."

In corner of the burial ground

They put him deep, and raised a mound

Of gravel o'er his cruel head;

And set a slab to mark his bed.

And when the obsequies were over,

Their common foe "well under cover,"

These likely six young Hampton men,

Who had to Hampton come again,
Assembled to recall their childhood;
And how they struggled through youth's wild
   wood.
Met in large hall of mansion old,
Their various experiences they told;
How ill they fared, and then how well;
What troubles and what luck befell.

THE GROUP.

One Alfred Atherton was there,
And David Williams, who offered prayer;
And Samuel Crane, of course a Smith;
And tall and slim was William Wythe.
Brave John Jameson, inclined to rhymes,
Possessed a heart for stirring times.

Then John they choose to tell in verse,

In easy, off-hand, style rehearse,

His life throughout the six years past

Since they were met together last.

But Jameson modestly preferred

This story of himself deferred,

And told instead, in rythmic plan,

How Goodman, Hampton's noblest man,

Great honors on the humble laid,

And for himself new honors made.

PART II.

JAMESON'S STORY.

THE WAYNES.

IN Hampton William Wayne abode,
   A noble soul, with heavy load
Of poverty and want to bear.
Harry, his son, inured to care,
Most kindly to his burdens took,
And nobly did an insult brook.
Wayne's special foe Flint Sternman was,
Whose skill at meanness did surpass
All aspirants for chiefest fame

JAMESON'S STORY.

At building up a tyrant name.

To Sternman luck a mortgage brought,

On Wayne's homestead good, and naught

That Wayne proposed could move the man

To diverge from his dastard plan,

To foreclose on the little cot,

And all the Waynes from Hampton blot.

One hundred dollars treasured well,

Young Wayne to fee at school "a spell,"

Was sacrificed to Sternman's wrath;

And, still, to clear them from his path,

There wanted just two hundred more;

And Sternman, at the cottage door,

The Waynes from Hampton "warned" away,

Upon a gloomy autumn day,

When Johnnie Wayne, a lovely boy,

The household's pet, and pride, and joy,

O'erworked in weather cold and wet,

To aid in lessening the debt,

Was dead within.

The father crazed went wandering west,

In vaguest searching after rest.

The mother sought some distant friends,

And planned for loss to make amends.

And Harry Wayne, ah! shut the page;

Of misery he lived an age

In one short year; and, left alone,

He earned his bread about the town.

Yet darkness but precedes the light;

The darkness deep—the morning's bright.

WAR DAYS COME.

When April suns and softening showers
Blessed Hampton hearts and Hampton bowers,
The rebel war burst on the land,
And patriot hearts were beating grand!
John Goodman's regiment was raised
When first the Southern war news blazed.
The county sent a thousand strong,
To die or sing the victor's song;
In Hampton's hundred Harry Wayne,
The bravest of the hundred men.
But he lacked cash, and was too meek,
For recognition fit, to seek.
To Sternman's son command was given;
And, as I hope at last for heaven,
So small, so mean, and austere man

The earth had not since time began.
The father was considered bad,
But greater tyrant was the lad.

"DO THOU, MY HARRY."

This disappointment as to place
Wayne bore with very perfect grace,
And soon received a word of cheer
From one his heart held very dear,
A gentle girl, with habit plain,
Whose pretty name was Mary Mayne:
"Do thou, my Harry, musket take;
With that thy noble record make.
Thy talents well deserve a sword,
But, treasure up my parting word,
If well thou serve thou mayest command,

And yet be honored through the land.
And every day the sun doth rise,
My waking and my closing eyes
Shall look to heaven, that not in vain
Doth suffer my good Harry Wayne."
And in this band, John Jameson said,
I followed where John Goodman led.
My comrade was this Harry true,
Whose story I discourse to you.
To torture Wayne and crush his heart
Was Captain Sternman's only art.
He deemed his noblest duty done,
If he abused this manly one.
The hardest task to Wayne he gave,
Regarding him ignoble slave.

COLONEL GOODMAN AND HIS MEN.

But Colonel Goodman, brave and kind,
Blessed with a noble, royal mind—
He was my model of a man;
Heaven forms them on no higher plan.
No man our regiment within
But deemed it were the grossest sin
To disobey the Colonel's word
Or rest when Goodman drew his sword.
Near fifty, then, but young and bright,
John Goodman was a well-built knight,
Of scarcely less than Titan height.
His hair and whiskers iron gray,
A trifle in the slouching way,
He wore his soldier chieftain's hat,
Which like a crown of glory sat.

Like quaint John Bunyan's good Great Heart
Was Goodman, skilled in all the art
Of nobly doing kindly deeds;
And if the record rightly reads,
So keen his sense of what was right,
He paused on horse in thickest fight,
To look his thanks for good deeds done,
And bravery by the humblest shown.
And wounded soldiers on the field,
Before their latest breath would yield,
If still they had the power to hear
When Goodman's voice rang sweet and clear,
Would rise with that reviving will
Which sometimes dying soldiers fill,
And fight with foe, and fight with death,
And in their struggles gain new breath;
And with their band the battle win,

Then help to bring the wounded in,
And find themselves had wounds.
And Goodman all the wounded nursed,
For when in luck the best and worst,
And at the last, as at the first,
For doing it if roundly cursed,
By officers of higher grade
Who wished no useless trouble made,
This Goodman cared for all his men,
And sought to bring them home again.
No wound but met his kindly eye,
And, did a sick man chance to die,
John Goodman knew the reason why;
And one brave heart was there to mourn,
And have the body homeward borne.
Such was the man whom Hampton sent
To lead her valiant regiment.

He wore the eagles to the wars
And graduated with two stars.
For rank he wisely held respect;
And so refrained to act direct
And Captain Sternman reprimand
For ruling with an iron hand
Whom he should lead, inspire and cheer,
And treasure all their interests dear.
But Goodman noted down with care
His tyranny, too great to bear,
And noted how young Harry took
Insults no other man could brook.

IN GOODMAN'S TENT.

Though long deferred, the wrath that came
Did not belie John Goodman's name;

Full two years after warring went
This Goodman brave, within his tent
A scene, when he has words to say
To Sternman for his tyrant way:

GOODMAN SPEAKS TO STERNMAN.

"In trials where no coward could,
And where I little thought he would,
Our Wayne has proved so truly good,
And firmly in the battle stood,
I often deeply wondered why:
'Did some sweet influence from the sky
Inspire the boy and cheer his heart
To nobly act a hero's part?'
Then thought it was in Hampton where
A sweet girl daily offered prayer,

That God would keep whom she had sent,
With musket, to my regiment.
And, Sternman, that choice Hampton girl,
By acts bespeaking you a churl,
You sought to win from Harry Wayne.
I think your wooing is in vain;
For, as I wear this trusty sword,
You shall return so much abhorred,
You cannot lisp the meekest word!
When swept the rebels round the ridge,
Wayne left his post to cut the bridge.
It sank in stream; they could not ford.
That night the chaplain thanked the Lord,
That through the providence of heaven
This quick deliverance was given.
But instrumental of this good
Our Harry Wayne, who understood,

He left his post at peril great,
If you administered his fate.
Ere Harry reached his picket place,
You, who are dependant on my grace,
As captain of the night rode round;
Harry, absent, then you found,
But from his post our Harry went
To save our good old regiment,
Resting, then, as it had right,
So tired and worn by march and fight.
I had a six-day furlough home,
And 'ere "old Goodman" back should come,'
This Wayne you clandestinely tried,
To get him sentenced, sir, you lied!
And thus the cruel record stood:
One day to carry log of wood,
And, for desertion, next, be shot.

And then you said, 'Will Mary Mayne,
I wonder, weep for Harry Wayne?'
Had I remained the furlough through
He had been hid from mortal view!
To-morrow execution day,
When you this Wayne would hide away!
There's Harry now with manly grace,
A patient meekness on his face,
Pacing near the guard-tent door,
His shoulders from the sentence sore.
Orderly bring him without harm,
Myself shall place upon his arm
This well-earned chevron, as a slight
Reward for all his acting right.
And, Sternman, here I make a vow,
Your dastard self to him shall bow,
And crave his pardon on the spot

That you have dug for Wayne to rot.

If more brave deeds this boy shall do,

A captain he; and major, too,

He'll be, ere this bad war is through.

And Captain Sternman quick resign;

We have no room for souls like thine;

Your tyrant conduct endeth here,

Your time has come to cringe with fear."

Then Sternman urged the deep disgrace,

And begged John Goodman's pardoning face:

"Had'st thou insulted me direct,

A pardon free might thou expect;

But that bad crime of tyranny,

To brave as Wayne has proved to be,

Transcends the power to mortals given,

And overtaxes gracious heaven.

JAMESON'S STORY.

I'll publish my official thanks,
That every soldier in the ranks,
Shall know so brave as Harry Wayne
Has not endured your wrath in vain;
Official thanks for doing that
For which you had him sentenced shot.
Two years upon his lot I wept,
And patiently my wrath have kept;
For respite, thus far, you may thank
Respect for military rank."

A MEMORABLE PARADE.

The regimental line was made,
To hold the formal dress parade;
And when the adjutant had read

John Goodman's thanks, so nobly said,

"Hail to the Chief," the soldiers sang,

And loudly then three brave cheers rang.

Then Harry Wayne so meek appears,

His eyes suffused with manly tears;

And cheer on cheer to Goodman's name

Well rounded out this scene of fame.

THE FIGHT AT SUNSET.

A courier swift across the plain—

"The foe are coming down amain!"

Straight Goodman's boys, with muskets bright,

Wheel into line and march to fight.

Led by this man of noble heart,

How Goodman's men ply well their art.

Then Sternman as a private fought,

JAMESON'S STORY.

And Wayne of no old grudges thought;
O'er Sternman hung a rebel stroke
And Harry then the sabre broke!
And sharp and loud the muskets rang,
And all the horrid, bloody clang
Of war the soldiers made,
And scores of killed and wounded laid.
At setting of the western sun
Was this successful fight begun;
'Twas at the darkened hour of ten
The rebels said, "we're conquered men."

"AND WITH HIS MUSKET EARNED A SWORD."

All honor be to Goodman's name;
By this sharp fight he gained new fame.
Soon shining stars his coat adorned;

And Harry Wayne, whom Sternman scorned,
A captaincy was duly given,
A gift well pleasing unto heaven.
The space of time was very brief,
Ere he acquired the yellow leaf;
Then braver he than e'er before,
His yellow leaf was silvered o'er;
Up honor's scale he quickly passed,
And gained the eagles at the last.
Then came the news about the tree,
Where meekly figured Robert Lee.
The hard-fought strife at last was through,
And after Johnson's grand review,
The Union men came from the wars,
In glory clad, and marked with scars.
Commander of the regiment,
In which he first a soldier went,

Wayne homeward rode, and gave his sword
To her whose brave and cheering word,
And prayers each day unto the Lord,
Were answered well, by Him who keeps
The truly brave and never sleeps.
So Harry proved how true her word,
And with his musket earned a sword.

HEAVEN'S BEST PLAN.

Soon Hampton's happy village bell,
Doth honeyed news of marriage tell.
And Harry Wayne, the barefoot boy,
With whom the plebeians thought to toy;
Brave Colonel Wayne, the gallant man,
Accepteth now of Heaven's plan
To be as good as mortals can.

And Mary Mayne, heroic one,
Who such a blessed work had done
At praying for the regiment
In which her Harry warring went—
She, too, accepts of Heaven's plan
To be as good as mortals can.
Our Wayne has been a Boston man,
But now in Hampton will reside,
He does not hold to roaming wide.

A TYRANT'S GRAVE.

When Sternman came in such disgrace,
No one in Hampton gave a place.
The village brats his presence spurned,
And Hampton canines, snarling, turned;
And then his bitter cup to fill

His father used him passing ill.
Young Sternman died two years ago,
Across his grave the bleak winds blow.
Near him we've laid his father down;
Let praises rise from all the town!

THE EFFECT.

The group arose, together sang,
The while that grand old mansion rang,

> "God moves in a mysterious way
>   His wonders to perform;
> He plants his footsteps in the sea
>   And rides upon the storm.
>
> His purposes will ripen fast,
>   Unfolding every hour;
> The bud may have a bitter taste,
>   But sweet will be the flower."

And then they sang "Old Hundred" so,

"Praise God from whom all blessings flow,"

That brave John Goodman, living by,

Thought he would call and ask them why

The noise; and, seeing Jameson there,

Entered and took the proffered chair;

And, greeting each, went on to say,

In Goodman's old great-hearted way,

What Hampton's future seemed to be;

How grand its coming history.

PART III.

GOODMAN TO THE GROUP.

EACH PLAN SUCCEEDS.

A THOUSAND things we think to do,
　　To make our old town grandly new;
Each plan succeeds; I can't tell how—
We're in the winning business now!
And now, young men, abide in town,
For through the wide world up and down,
There is no better, safer spot,
To build your fortune and your cot.

Good Farmer Dow, across the street,
With all his buildings large and neat,
And fruitful lands, and cash in bank;
And holding here good social rank,
A motto took in early life,
That proved of choicest blessings rife:
"Whoever fully plays his part,
Is always raking toward the cart!"

TEMPERANCE AT HAMPTON.

You may remember Peter Pyne,
Whom no man could redeem from wine.
This man has now a twelve-month served,
And never from the pledge has swerved.
One day the wily tavern man
Endeavored, as those rum men can,

To coax him to the tavern in,

And lead into his olden sin.

But Pyne so prayed there came a power

To help him in that trying hour.

He bravely then the luring spurned,

And from the tempter quickly turned.

Then sought my door all trembling white—

"General Goodman, I acted right!"

"Yes, Pyne, you have, and, noble friend,

I'll surely help you to the end.

To tempt a man who struggles so;

There is no blacker crime below."

I promptly made a little plan

And gave it to my servant man:

"You leave no piece of upright wood

Where this old Blaisdell's tavern stood;

Quick, Robert, pull this tavern down,

That has so cursed our pleasant town."
"And troth, yer honor, it's Robert that will,
And livil it flat as an auld dung-hill!"
So, calling out his Celtic son,
They made the rarest sort of fun,
At blotting out this Hampton hell,
And all the people said, "'tis well."
Now, after first good deeds are done,
We will not leave poor Pyne alone;
But grant him greeting, wish him health,
A home, and happiness, and wealth;
Bright flowers to see, fountains to hear;
And, in the merry time of year,
Some grand old rides in happy sleighs.
We'll try all generous-hearted ways,
That noble-minded men devise,
To help the sinning to the skies,

And make them happy on the earth,
And deem themselves as something worth;
Always we'll seek his heart to win,
Nor let him have the chance to sin,
But give him all good-tempered cheer,
And hope and joy, in place of fear.

A SCHOOL ON THE TAVERN SITE.

Soon where that old rum tavern stood,
We'll have, as every village should,
A school, where poorest boy may seek,
A knowledge of the tough old Greek,
And modern French and Latin grand,
And all the science in the land;
A knowledge gain of common sense,
And learn to think and act intense,

And have a heart that is immense.

The building done a three-month hence,

The opening term will then begin,

Luck we shall have, I think, therein.

You, Jameson, teach this Hampton school;

And keep it by no stingy rule.

The noblest boy shall head his class

Until another shall surpass,

In humble greatness, not in brass,

Nor yet in brains alone;

Naught shall by any means atone

For littleness!

Our Judge shall be good Harry Wayne,

Who's coming into town again.

David Williams, I think, will preach;

No better man the Word to teach.

Welcome there'll be for all, and place,
To exercise their gifts and grace.

GOOD NIGHT.

Now Goodman rose to take his leave;
Like children then these strong men grieve,
And press him sore to pass the night,
"For going home was hardly right."
But Goodman said: I seek my bower,
For soundeth from the village tower
The music of the midnight hour.
My friends, it seems from three till twelve,
Intent in memories to delve,
You have not taken rest nor food;
Such living is not for your good.
Excuse me now; but, by the way,

I heard our Farmer Dow to say—
And Thursday is Thanksgiving day—
"My General John, those six young men,
When they to Hampton come again,
Old Farmer Dow will feast them then,
And, General John, of course, you come,
And make yourself, and them, at home."
Thus we shall have our turkey sweet
At Mr. Dow's, across the street.

PART IV.

AT THE THANKSGIVING.

THE old New England feast had come,
    In Mr. Dow's substantial home;
And kith and kin of Farmer Dow,
Unwed or with the marriage vow;
And young and old, a great array,
Were gathered on that festal day.
John Goodman there, with his young men,
Appeared himself, a youth, again.
Mr. and Mrs. Harry Wayne,
Attired in habit rich but plain,

Arrived upon the Boston train,

Inquiring for the health and gain,

Of all assembled at that board,

With Mrs. Dow's provision stored.

Then grace was said and praise was sung,

But brief they talked of pies and tongue:

For Goodman still had words to say,

In Goodman's old great-hearted way,

What Hampton's future seemed to be,

How grand its coming history:

THE FACTORIES.

"Two mills are done, and soon a third;

They grow like magic at our word.

Strong cotton goods in one are made;

In others, prints that will not fade.

AT THE THANKSGIVING.

A paper-mill shall be our boast,
Erected at a heavy cost;
Built strong, correct, from defects clear,
Supplied with finest Fourdrinier,
Whereon three tons of every grade
Of writing papers—wove and laid—
Shall be produced, and shipped, and sold,
To bring us handy heaps of gold.
Fine paper collars shall be made;
And it shall be a noble trade.
So beautiful the shop shall be,
From dust, and mould, and litter free,
That people from afar shall come,
And bring some member of their home
To work within so choice a place,
And learn the way to work with grace.
And, called to toil by silver gong,

The operatives, happy throng,
Shall pass the village street along,
Vexing the air with pleasant song!

THE HAMPTON PAPER.

The town now has a weekly sheet,
Quite newsy, smart, and printed neat;
And all right glad its pages greet.
But, as we have our railroad through,
I think we'll print a daily, too;
Wherein to give the wheat of news,
And verses worthy to peruse;
Neat editorials, short and smart,
On commerce, politics and art—
All richest things from raciest pen;
Our aim to help deserving men.

AT THE THANKSGIVING.

Flint Sternman's homestead is the place
Where, by the aid of gospel grace,
We'll print our paper, dedicate
To all that makes our Hampton great;
And Harry Wayne, and Jameson, too,
Who are prepared this work to do,
Shall write upon this newsy sheet,
For such arrangement will be meet.

A CHURCH AND A LODGE.

Though Masonry in Hampton 's new,
I think we'll have a lodge in blue,
And Harry shall be master, too.
And soon we'll consummate a plan
To honor Christ and honor man;
A Christian church, as heaven designed,

In which all Christian sects are joined.

And Williams shall the pastor be,

An earnest, pious preacher he.

In Sabbath school we all intend

A constant helping hand to lend,

But Harry Wayne must superintend.

Most modest man, who earned a sword

By trusting maiden and the Lord;

True soldier brave, my model man,

Who suffered as no coward can,

Unknown in youth—now take the van!"

WITH ALL THESE HONORS.

With all these honors on his head,

Brief were the words that Harry said:

"There's such a change 'twixt now and then,

AT THE THANKSGIVING.

From plebeian scorn to praise by men!
I little dreamed of joy like this;
Heaven grant the grace t' endure the bliss;
And teach me how the good to keep
By aiding those who want and weep.
Henceforth I trust and bless my kind;
And in that trust my blessing find."
Then Jameson spoke his gratitude,
And David Williams, tall and good;
When Goodman gave a brief reply,
As evening time was drawing nigh:
"Of joy so filled, I wish to shout,
And let the pent-up glory out;
As Methodist I might surpass
The bravest Wesley in his class!
Bring hither all who want our aid,
On whom life's heavy woes are laid;

Who wish our prayers that heaven will bless,

Our hand to lift them from distress;

To aid them all we make our vow;

We're in that sort of business now!"

MRS. JOHN GOODMAN.

"The sweetest wife, my mild Marie,

Is sixty now, and so am I.

Two children died long years ago,

With typhus fever deep and slow;

The angels sent a bird again,

A manly boy, now five and ten.

Wife prayed for me through all the wars,

And gloried in my sword and scars;

In rebel and the Mexic fight,

Her faith has kept my armor bright.

A tender eye she hath for poor
Who seek a blessing at our door.
One day she said, "'Tis not a task
To grant the favor that I ask;
You have three hundred thousand, just,
Secured by honest means, I trust;
Give me a full five thousand down,
With gig to ride about the town.'
Some generous scheme I knew she planned
To bless the needy of the land;
Nor closer then the details scanned,
Enough that wife could understand;
But drew the check, a phaeton bought,
A gentle steed from 'York State' brought;
And, loaded well with baskets down,
She drives her team about the town,
Dispensing blessings to the poor,

Who have not now to seek our door!"
And thus with pride full worthy youth,
This silvered man, in sincere truth,
Discoursed of plans with which his wife
Was nobly rounding out her life.

BREAD ON THE WATERS.

In answer to an urgent call
From each within the festive hall,
John Jameson gave a story brief,
Concerning which they had belief
He knew full well, and figured, too,
As benefactor prompt and true;
And yet, so urged, what could he do
But honest tell the story through?
"How good returns our labors bring;

Strange as the themes the weird bards sing;

One man I know was grand but wild;

Romantic man when but a child.

In after years this man, again,

I met among the comely men

Who thronged the porch, a pleasant place

Where prayer, and praise, and words of grace,

Gave sacred charm and hallowed joy,

The choicest bliss and no alloy.

At first I could not trust my eyes;

But he confirmed my glad surprise.

More than a year he owned the Lord,

And trusted in his heavenly word.

And then to others, there, he said:

'This man for me devoutly prayed

In tent upon the Southern glade,

When, wretched, scoffing, steeped in sin,

I baffled all his work to win.

And then he saved my earthly life,

When we were marching from the strife.

And I was sick, and sank to die,

Beneath that fervid Southern sky.

He spoke the noblest words of cheer,

Which even now I freshly hear;

He gave me drink, my musket bore,

And, to the firm land took me o'er

The miasmatic swamp, that teemed

With death, and like my nature seemed;

And, by the side of spreading tree,

He spoke of home and Christ to me.

We joined, at last, the army train,

And had the luck the camp to gain.

When war was done and I returned,

Good wisdom's teachings still I spurned;

But though most reckless I have been,
God's wondrous grace has saved from sin.'
And more he would have said, but there
The preacher rose to offer prayer.
We passed from vestibule to pew,
And of God's grace, forever new,
The preacher taught the blessed plan
Designed to save rebellious man.
How blest that Sabbath day to me;
How great its influence shall be!
A blessed evening hour we passed;
The first, but not the best nor last.
This friend for bread did run a mill,
By limpid lake, at foot of hill,
Whose cheerful din is with me still.
And near the mill sequestered grot;
Hard by the dell, a pleasant cot,

Wherein his wife so sweet and young,
Her cheerful joy, enraptured sung;
And childish song, with tender art,
Burst forth from one delighted heart.
A charm around the scene was thrown,
The prosy world has never known.
He prospers still, and God have praise
For all his many happy days."

"WITH CIRCUMSPECTION, LET US, NOW."

As though far off an angel sung,
Through all the room a stillness hung.
Then Goodman rose, with reverence said—
A saintly glory on his head:—
"With circumspection, let us, now,
Before the Benefactor bow,

From whom all blessings flow to men,

And pray and praise his name again."

With bursting hearts, and face joy-limned,

Their final praise they sweetly hymned;

And then to Dame and Farmer Dow,

Each neighbor made no formal bow,

But said, "For you choice good we ask,

Much be your joy, and kind your task!

And we ourselves now dedicate

To help men to a happy state,

And by such means make Hampton great!"

WHEN GOODMAN DIES.

Sincerely hoping, in my song,

That brave John Goodman liveth long,

Yet still, as all must pass away,

AT THE THANKSGIVING.

There cometh on a requiem day,
When General John must leave his sword
And rise, to meet and praise his Lord.
Ah! that will be no idle throng,
That crowd the village street along;
Each home will have a sadder song,
And e'en the merry eyes among,
The sigh will break, the tear will start,
And honest sorrow move each heart.
The regiment will gather there,
The parson say no formal prayer,
And citizens, and soldiers, too,
Will weep as brave for brave men do!

OUR YANKEE LAND.

OUR YANKEE LAND.

GOD bless the good New England hills,
   And every valley there;
God bless the mountain lakes and brooks,
   And their salubrious air.
And choicest blessings rest upon
   The people of those States;
God grant them pleasant skies above,
   With plenty at their gates.

Prosperity attend their toil,
   In factory and field;
And may their skill with car and ship
   Abundant profit yield.
May pestilence and famine spare

This most delightful spot ;
And distant be the day when crime
Its history shall blot.

Although appeareth sectional,
To sing New England's praise,
I point the nation's history,
Through dark and prosperous days,
For proof that our New England leads
In national affairs,
And, with ability and grit,
The nation's burdens bears.

So, then, full fearlessly, with joy,
Whatever banner flaunt ;
Do rebel Southrons greet with scorn,
Or Britons with a taunt ;

We'll sing their name, whose head and heart,
    And never-faltering hand,
Have well upheld the stars and stripes—
    God bless our Yankee land.

Oh could I be forgiven, did
    My heart not turn to thee,
With gratitude and pride, dear land,
    For all thou art to me:
Thine atmosphere and scenery,
    Thy present, future, past;
Thy trials first, and glory now,
    To last while time shall last?

God bless the land where I was born,
    And played, a happy child,
Ere yet I saw a southern swamp,

Or roamed a western wild;
And where, within a cot among
　　Our Massachusetts hills,
My early being was attuned
　　By cadence of the rills.

And, in the future of my life,
　　Where'er my pathway lies;
Whatever lot is meted out,
　　Or kind, or cold my skies,
Still evermore, my song, at home
　　Or on a foreign strand,
Through life, and at the honest hour,
　　God bless our Yankee land!

LOCAL LINES.

THE DEAD DOHERTY.

"LET Erin weep; my Bridget's dead!"
  Said Doherty, one day;
"Ye Celtic braves bewail her all,
  And Praste O'Connor pray.
Then round the corpse, for carnival,
  Assemble with your wine,
To mark her exit from the world
  With drunkenness divine!

"The sober Yankee race may deem
  Such business grossest sin;
But Irishmen have royal right
  To aid their grief with gin!

From sighs to sips of mourning grog
　　Our hearts shall alternate;
And does a Yankee dare protest,
　　We'll break his worthless pate.

"So light the candles round her, now,
　　And drink unto her joy,
That she may quickly pass where hell
　　Can never more annoy!
Brave is the way the Irish die,
　　And grand the funeral rite,
Where sober men are not allowed,
　　Nor those afraid to fight!

"And as through purgatory walks
　　The spirit of my wife,

THE DEAD DOHERTY.

Drink once, again, and then prepare
   To wage a holy strife.
Hit hard and sharp, my lively lads,
   A glorious battle make;
Then drink again, and swear and fight—
   Such is the Irish wake!"

The happy Irishmen I know
   Must not surmise they're hit—
The pleasant Emeraldic men
   Of common sense and wit;
Who manifest in ways and words
   Urbanity and grit;
Unto whose inoffensive lives
   My satire would not fit.

"SAM'S" PAPER.

"SAM" run a paper in the town
    With such consummate tact,
I am inclined to give, in rhyme,
    My memories of the fact.

This leading journal's columns teemed
    With "'tisements," "eds," and news,
And fearlessly, therein, with force,
    Our Samuel spoke his views

On politics or church affairs,
    And things of social life;
And if he wished to "smash" a man,
    He waged a royal strife.

"SAM'S" PAPER.

A kind assistant had the charge
   Of such rhetoric truck
As to the office came, with prayers
   It might be blessed with luck,

He was with mild pretensions blest,
   With wit and great good sense,
With power that ran in even course,
   And not in fits intense.

An energetic business man
   The printing contracts made;
Episcopalian in his creed,
   And science at his trade.

He was a wit of upper rank,
   None handier than he

To perpetrate a healthy joke,
   Or timely repartee.

Shrewd in the line of news and things,
   The chiefest local man,
To gather in occurrences,
   Had very happy plan.

And all the inward coming trains
   Bore missives crammed with news,
From voting for the governor
   To rental of church pews.

A clever critic was attached,
   Whose criticisms smacked
More of the good a book possessed,
   Than of the good it lacked.

For many years, successfully
    Toiled on this able force;
Their journal praised and envied, too,
    For its most prosperous course.

In later days division came
    A quartette went away,
To run a lively evening sheet;
    And made the business pay.

OUR CONDUCTORS.

POLITE and careful, to the "Hub"
   John moves his morning cars;
At evening brings them home again,
   When early blink the stars.

Through fretting days of summer hot,
   In winter, spring, or fall,
He takes your tickets with good grace,
   Your questions answers all.

Commanders of our lightning train,
   To whom the gods impart
The grace to run our swiftest cars,
   How difficult the art,

OUR CONDUCTORS.

From Boston to the Hudson, far,
   Through cut, and gorge, and glen,
Along the streams and o'er the hills,
   With angel speed and ken,

Two hundred passengers to bear,
   As on divans at rest;
Connecting at the Alban point
   With lightning coaches, west!

And bravely hence, unto the sound
   The noonday train is driven;
Well fitted for the place, the man
   To whom command is given.

A man who drives noon coaches south,
   Where Woronoco lays,

For courage, skill, and constancy,
　　Deserves our hearty praise.

Like music in an even song,
Our old conductor, tall and strong,
For years has run his train along

The railway up the mountain route,
Where road and river wind about,
And beetling cliffs stand jagged out.

From valley, up the hights, away,
To where Fort Orange greets the day,
His changeless, constant route doth lay.

And up the grade by morning light,
And down the grade, again, at night,
His course has been, three decades quite.

THE "RIVER ROAD."

IN joyous spring or winter cold,
    And in the autumn sun,
The trains upon our northern route
    With good success are run.

And, bound to Methodistic camp,
    Or going mountainward,
On picnics bent, or politics,
    The people with accord

Declare they like the "River road,"
    Its managers and men;
And when they wish another ride,
    They'll try that route again.

And so the pleasant "tunnel route"
 Is worthy well a line,
For able, thorough, management;
 For scenery grand and fine.

SUMMER PLACES.

BARRINGTON.

WHEN next the heated term returns,
    And high the summer solstice burns,
Our hearts shall find serene delight
In breezes on some Berkshire hight;
Or by that pleasant winding stream,
Whose waters 'neath the willows gleam,
The Housatonic river, blest,
Whose pleasant murmur giveth rest.
With proper prepäration done,
We'll drive away to Barrington;
A town with grandest mountain charms,
And most delightful valley farms;
Where city folk the summer pass
Amid the maples and the grass;

Where people have a royal way
In all their deeds and all they say;
The home of cultured men of note,
That fine old town where Bryant wrote,
And Russell delved and earned his gold,
Nor from the poor did wealth withhold;
And Leavitt lives 'mid paintings rare;—
A town where river, hill, and air,
And pleasant vale, and storied glen,
And noble homes of noble men,
Bespeak a fit resort for kings
Or they who come to us on wings.

TILDEN.

Near "the Junction," far up north,
　　Are many scenes of rarest worth.
Across the river, "high and dry,"
Upon a mountain, toward the sky,
The Tilden school, known through the land,
With edifice, complete and grand,
Where women learn selectest truth,
To bless them in the days of youth,
Equip them for the work of life,
And prove of choicest blessings rife.
Around this school the pleasant scene
Shall ever be in memory green.
To learners there, blest evermore

Be hill, and dale, and willowed shore;

The bridge that spans the river o'er;

And all the scenery grand and wild,

Of rock and hill profusely piled.

UP THE PASSUMPSIC.

ALONG the verdant upland plains,
    How pleasant run Passumpsic trains;
By beechen grove and rocky glen,
And storied haunt of Indian men;
By cosy farm, 'neath craggy hill,
And busy, fragrant lumber mill;
A singing, plashing water-fall,
And clump of moaning blackwood tall;
Trim alders by the purling brook,
And sugar maples in the nook,
Whence fleecy smoke and joyous shout
In early spring comes floating out;
And ample fields of ripening maize,
And orchards rich on autumn days;

And roads where drive the happy sleighs,

When brave King Boreas grandly plays—

Along the northern vales and plains,

How pleasant run Passumpsic trains.

"ISRAEL'S RIVER."

STILL farther north a pleasant vale,
    Where " Israel's River " singeth well;
Where noble hills the vale surround,
And men of chivalry are found,
Whose impulses are like the god's;
Who do brave deeds, whate'er the odds.
The village is the county seat,
Where lawyers for their business meet;
Yet quiet and delightful town,
In summer and when summer 's flown;
So grandly winter holds his sway,
The people have a regal way;
And pity much the dwellers where
They never know the northern air,

But pine beneath the southern skies
In lowlands where diseases rise.
Within this vale of Lancaster,
How pleasant summer sunsets are;
How sweet the rays fall on the hills,
On cottage, river, glen and rills.
Within this happy northern vale
My summer visit shall not fail.
In walks the warbling streams along,
With joy induced by their calm song,
My days shall pleasant come and go,
As brooklets over pebbles flow.
In converse with the noble men
Who bless these homes and know each glen,
I shall surmise on earth, again,
The sainted have returned to dwell,
And of the upper regions tell,

"ISRAEL'S RIVER."

Which Lancaster, in hill and dell,
And stream and sky, doth equal well.
There happy be the marriage bell;
Infrequent sound the funeral knell;
Nor iron fact the bard compel
To sing that evil luck befell
The place where men and gods combine
To build a town of grand design.

THE AMMONOOSUC.

IN autumn days and summer suns,
   How wild the Ammonoosuc runs,
'Mid varied scene of bold rocks, tall,
And plunging, dashing waterfall.
Next, far receding, craggy dell;

Anon a fertile intervale;

And then, to use the plunging flood,

Is busy mill on ledges stood,

For things of grain, or leather good,

Or articles carved out of wood.

Then southward pass, and travel back,

Along the pleasant Merrimac;

And through the grand old Granite State,

New England, all, so small, yet great,

We learn from car, and mill, and mine,

And dwelling built of neat design,

Our land has greatness from the fact,

That, perseveringly, with tact,

Its sons improve resources given;

While special blessings come from heaven

To crown their labors, and to fill

Their homes with good, hewn by their skill.

www.ingramcontent.com/pod-product-compliance
Lightning Source LLC
Chambersburg PA
CBHW021948160426
43195CB00011B/1282